# Beautiful Imperfections

# BEAUTIFUL IMPERFECTIONS

T.C. MONK

Published 2023

# Other Works by Author

~<u>Poetry</u>~
∴

Imperfections of Beauty
(Book 1)

`<u>Sci-Fi</u>`
∴

Lumen's Quiddity
('Pariah' series)

=

Daedal Convergence
[Book 2]

=

Orphic Dénouement
[Book 3 – Due out late 2027]

-<u>Philosophy</u>-
∴

The Ties That Bind

⸮<u>Prison/Nonfiction</u>⸮
∴

T.O.M.B.
(Those of My Blood)

'<u>Fiction</u>'
∴

Velvet Smoke

=

Beyond The Veil

'<u>Erotica</u>'
∴

Masculine Shadows

# Dedication

The collection of work in this volume is dedicated to my family, who stood by me through my turbulent young life and supported me in their own way, regardless of the distance between us.

# Contents

# Acknowledgments

I want to acknowledge the following individuals for their support of this creation and the time they invested in bringing it to life.

Linda Mack, for all her astute attention to detail and dedication to helping those who desire to help themselves.

My brother, for believing in me enough to take the time out of his life to help me re-craft the one I ruined at such a young age.

The students and faculty interns of 'The Pen Project' classes (2022/2023) taught in the School of Humanities, Arts, and Cultural Studies at Arizona State University's West Campus.

# Author's Note

N.B.: This work includes four poems with specific design parameters meant to be highlighted for the readers. The titles of the poems F.T.F.I.G.L. and N.I.K.M. are revealed by reading down the left side of the piece itself. The poem 'Imagenigma' can be read from top to bottom and bottom to top. 'Built to Shine,' part one, appears in 'Imperfections of Beauty' in the series.

# 'BEAUTIFUL IMPERFECTIONS,'
## 2022

In the garden of benevolent love,
the heart blooms like a delicate flower,
velvet shades color its petals,
feral passion feeds its power.

Among the arbor of vicious hate,
a sickness breeds within its womb,
its sinister shadow spins a snare,
weaving a web meant to entomb.

Along the journey of autonomous choice,
the mind fashions the will of progress,
its story builds the path of freedom,
the pages of history laud success.

Within the glass of measured amber,
the grains of life build a shrine,
an eternal monument made of death,
buried beneath the sands of time.

All the pleasures of life and death,
brede the flames of love and hate,
but when it comes to freedom and will,
the wheel of chance is choice and fate.

# 'DEATH'S STONE,' 2021

(Can You Guess What am I ?)


How strums the dull orchestra of time,
its resounding ballad sung in silence,
alone, it haunts the darkened castell,
the ichorous slave condemned to violence.


'Tis the piper without dues,
the lonely pauper none shall cheat,
its solemn life but seldom touched,
in the darkness of its keep.


Madness be its subtle caress,
delicate measures mete its rhythm,
its fervent passion sets the tone,
driving its devilish treason.

# 'THE EYE OF VOLK,' 1993

We are the keepers of purity and faith,
the champions of those who test our mettle,
the truest conviction of a proud Asatruar,
are those who fall in love with the struggle.


The true of heart show their quality,
keeping their mind and spirit true,
they never bend and never sway,
nor break like others do.


Purity of heart, strength of valor,
these are the tenets to which I hold,
honor, faith, integrity of heart,
these are the medals I wear like gold.


I will carry my banner, be it my charge,
and lead by example with strength evermore,
sing the praises of the living who die,
and pay homage to those who've come before.

# 'A LIMPID MOMENT,' 2004

Love can be lonely across the currents of time,
like a single ripple among the mighty sea.
Its solemn journey seeking distant shores,
to wash upon sands of crystal and glass.
The mirror in the sky displays our world,
reflecting the elements and quiddity of life.
Rays of the morning cast shadows of the Sun,
creating waves of euphoria to temper our lives.
Born in an instant and dying too fast,
among the calamity of an immaculate storm.
Fading to oblivion among the seething aether
is a dirge-like cadence heralding our swan song.
The theater of the mind reflects only the past,
which creates illusions to preserve our sanity.

# 'LORDS OF KARMA,' 2021

Camouflaged rock clips his shoe.
He stumbles,
grasping for purchase,
no net,
nothing but air.
He falls forward,
the puddle smacks his face.
Hacking dollops of grainy spittle,
he curses the villainous stone.
Droplets,
like ruby wine,
dye the mere,
dripping freely from his brow.


A dark creature scurries from its hovel,
eight legs bounding dauntlessly forward,
water-walking like a god,
come to claim its victuals.


Body shifting,
hands jerk fearfully,
muddy water displaces with force.
The intrepid minikin is repelled,
the micro tsunami sweeps it away.

Standing,
staring,
heart's a riot.
Wet like a soaked rag,
for want to scream,
he digresses,
defeated,
embarrassed...
beyond consolation.

His getaway sticks bear him onward,
kicking,
stomping,
a Bairn's fret.
Sour virulence curls his lip,
for spider,
water,
...and cursed stone.

# 'A SIMPLE SOLUTION,' 1998

Imagine me without limitation.
Understand me without explanation.
Support me without fail.
Keep me without prohibition.
Believe me beyond doubt.
Adore me beyond compare.
Crave me beyond imagination.
Covet me beyond ambition.
Hold me in every dream.
Feel me in every breeze.
See me in every smile.
Honor me in every deed.
Take me as I am.

# 'THINGS OF JOY,' 2018

Tears of comfort bereft of pain,
desire that burns within the vein.
A simple touch, what is given,
the shame of hate once it's forgiven.
The pleasures of sin, the cravings we feed,
passion that brings us to our knees.
Fields of lavender, oceans of gold,
the solace found in songs of old.
A mind enthralled, a heart set free,
the rhythm of love beyond its melody.
Bonds of youth, the chasing game,
are 'Things of Joy' we share the same.

The hint of rain upon the wind,
the fragrant scent of nature's skin.
A shooting star, an intimate wish,
the aphrodisiac of a soughing kiss.
Stolen moments fraught with sentiment,
the intrepid heart of the innocent.
A warming smile, the sweetest prize,
the comely attitude in some snug Levi's.
The rising Sun, the sultry Moon,
beautiful sights to set the mood.
Ambrosial flowers, the morning glow,
are 'Things of Joy' to soothe the soul.

Spring showers, the leaves of Fall,
Summer games, a Winter's ball.
The fountain of youth beyond the climb,
creation's waters to reset time.
The silent poet of beauty's heart,
hope within the candle's arc.
Holding hands, arm-in-arm,
the sultry duet of love's charm.
A new chapter, another memoir,
life woven from a quelling star.
An olive branch, laurels of Greece,
are 'Things of Joy' that foster peace.

Fruits of labor, fortune, and fame,
the gypsy wind inviting change.
Fields, mountains, rivers for miles,
the inherent nature in the call of the wild.
Forests of blooms in heaven's bower,
the breath of eternity beyond its hour.
Knowing the secret of God's desire,
an ardent passion to fear and admire.
Consumed by grace, seasonal rebirth,
the cold chased away by the blazing hearth.
Strength, love, friends with contrast
are 'Things of Joy' we build to last.

# 'THINGS OF PAIN,' 2018

Heartache and loss beyond consolation,
tears that fall without numeration.
Misplaced trust, a broken vow,
love that lives beyond the now.
A family broken by divorce,
callous words without remorse.
A selfish deed, sins of guilt,
coveting things that others built.
Lies that spurn, faiths that betray,
a specious scene in mortality's play.
Constant blame, a living tragedy,
are 'Things of Pain' contrived by calamity.

Passion lost, innocence taken,
the fear of trust once forsaken.
An absence felt within the heart,
freedom lost from the very start.
Silent shame, an open wound,
anguish woven by an empty womb.
A careless sibling, an absent parent,
maturing solo as an abstract fragment.
The sorrow of living a life alone,
a sufferance felt deep in the bone.
A tangled web, sinister lies,
are 'Things of Pain' encumbering our lives.

Smiles that lie, joys that kill,
comfort taken by those who will.
Words that sharpen the razor's edge,
phrases which push us over the ledge.
Hope once lost, freedom constrained,
the view beyond the windowpane.
Doubts that fester within the mind,
weave threads of terror like a creeping vine.
A lonely heart, a moment lost,
destiny woven upon the cross.
A whip, a curse, a thorny crown,
are 'Things of Pain' to break us down.

A measure of need, an ounce of hate,
the laughter beyond heaven's gate.
The tortured plea for another breath,
watching one's family laid to rest.
An unseen malady, a shadow inside,
the invisible sickness the body hides.
A child's cry, a parent's disdain,
the torment contrived by our fame.
Being at the mercy of another's will,
that which is taken by a poison pill.
The moments of life, agony we tolerate,
are 'Things of Pain' we all calculate.

# 'THINGS OF COMFORT,' 2018

A soft smile behind gentle eyes,
a painted sunset beyond the rise.
A father's pride, a mother's kiss,
wages of value we must possess.
The shining stars beyond the gloom,
their subtle delight is made for two.
A warming fire, the comforting wind,
pleasures shared with family and friends.
Puppy dog ears and kitten purrs,
joys that come from stroking their fur.
The hope we give, the love we receive,
are 'Things of Comfort' we all need.

The glowing candle within the dark,
a reassuring touch to comfort the heart.
Tears of laughter, eyes that shine,
the soothing charm of a meaningful rhyme.
A fear that vanishes before the rush,
the promise of forgiveness is a living trust.
Graceful psalms, inspiring themes,
shame that fades beyond the dream.
Poetic phrases to color one's mood,
lyrical tenses that conjure the muse.
The blessings offered, prayers we speak,
are 'Things of Comfort' we all seek.

Dreams of more beyond the stars,
a life of meaning bereft of scars.
Beautiful memories, songs of old,
the minstrel's spirit to excite the soul.
A missive within the hollow glass,
contain words of solace from the past.
Feelings of grace, a sense of pride,
meaningful measures the heart provides.
A cleansing rain to restore the view,
braids the arc of life renewed.
A cozy blanket, a familiar scent,
are 'Things of Comfort' and compliment.

The crowning halo of breaking dawn,
bears the light of morning's song.
A caring embrace, a look of favor,
sentimental thoughts we tend to savor.
Feelings that craft a parting wish,
ferrying emotions beyond the rift.
Helpful hints, a lucky clue,
to solve the riddle within the queue.
The voice of reason to still the mind,
winding back the hands of time.
Gifts of hope, a love of need,
are 'Things of Comfort' that set us free.

# 'THINGS OF SHAME,' 2018

Wicked themes our minds possess,
sinful thoughts we never confess.
Shrouded pain, shame that's hidden,
regretful words once they're given.
A needful lie to keep one safe,
forges the path of our own disgrace.
Feigned smiles, a joy that kills,
an accusing voice buried in the hills.
Fear that manifests among the night,
a child's tears woven by fright.
A shady past, a venial sin,
are 'Things of Shame' we hide within.

Comfort that's lost to forceful lust,
hope that vanishes with an unwanted touch.
A cruel heart, an empty hand,
the callus act of a vengeful plan.
Fangs that feed upon one's skin,
a rope that strangles the next of kin.
An absent parent, a child scorned,
feelings of remorse for being born.
Agony shackled like a demon bound,
plagues the mind with a sinister crown.
Poisonous pills, a desirous end,
are 'Things of Shame' we all comprehend.

Prophets who preach a faith they chide,
weaving their tenets in a web of lies.
A broken vow, a quieting hush,
predators that prey on pious trust.
Religious hypocrites who hide their wickedness,
behind a veil of venal sickness.
Sacrificial lambs, paradise lost,
upon the altar, we pay the cost.
The pleasures of vice are a mortal test,
a shared indulgence to feed our flesh.
A rite of passage, a cardinal sin,
are 'Things of Shame' that brand our skin.

Eyes that trace the curves of fantasy,
sets the stage for our depravity.
Impure thoughts, perverse views,
taboo desires the mind pursues.
Iniquitous measures are things we invite,
to nourish the soul with subtle delights.
Wanton rage, crimes of violence,
a sea of filth smothered by silence.
To test one's limits against the leather,
the ties that bind become our tether.
Virtues we shun, vices we praise,
are 'Things of Shame' that build our cage.

# 'EQUAL MEASURES,' 2001

HOPE guides us through the night
by midnight stars that glitter bold,
toward the land of the midnight sun
beyond compassion, sympathy, and sorrow.

FAITH secures us through the day
like the string between the pearls,
a measure to strengthen a weak resolve
in this dreary, hateful world.

COURAGE carries us when we fall
upon the wings of heaven's sparrow,
along the path of sacrifice,
to join the faithful of old.

DESIRE leads us along the trail
through the mist, fog, and snow,
where the road becomes obscured
and the heart falls to sorrow.

HONOR corrects us when we stray
and sets the truth within our sight,
it binds the hands of vengeance
and keeps our soul free of strife.

STRENGTH feeds our dormant virtue
and confines us beyond the fire,
holding the flames of hate at bay
and revenge beyond desire.

LOVE breeds in the hearts of all
a message within the dye,
its future becomes enigmatic
cloaked in mystery's guise.

DESPAIR is the cry of battered souls
those who suffer the right to live,
from within the well of sacrifice
are the wicked yet to give.

DOUBT fills us with unholy needs
ones that spawn our evil desires,
to wrap the innocent in crimson wings
with flames from the lake of fire.

FEAR drives us through the night
toward shadows beyond the veil,
to places of death and torment
where dead men tell no tales.

GREED can be a wicked road
one that reveals our savage guilt,
it feeds the need for us to covet
the things that others built.

SHAME is for those who need forgiveness
and those who seek redemption,
but in a world filled with sin
retribution has become our weapon.


WEAKNESS can be a fallow crutch
for those who seek asylum,
a refuge to keep them safe
from the violent world around them.


HATE can be the driving tool
for those who seek a thrill,
a compelling force that comforts
or a spur for one to kill.

# 'LUMINARY,' 2020

Awakening, emerging silent,
cometh the herald of morn,
the future's ward of making,
its spirit a salient storm.


Savage, its breath sows violence,
the oracle of paradise lost,
a quate Seraph of Providence,
enchanting, arresting the encroaching frost.


Luciferous, sacred prophet,
a Muse bound and divine,
the aureate coronet of morning,
a cosmic sentinel among its shrine.


Gravid, its touch be seminal,
a silent emblematic metronome,
the constant affluent hybrid
plaiting life's ineffable poem.

# 'SMITTEN,' 2022

A subtle presence draws the eye,
graceful,
she moves among the Lea.
A faint titter precedes her,
with curious eyes,
I am arrested.

Upon the ground, I sit,
back resting against a tree.
Nervously, I shiver,
like a timid child.

Grace pervades her dainty steps.
Her visual beauty fills my cup,
exceedingly,
hunger plagues me.

She sees me,
her smile like the sun,
it smites me,
murdering my resolve.
My stomach rebels,
sweat fills my palms.

Touch her,
I yearn to,
a million thoughts strangle me,
wishing she knew her power,
how wistful eyes drink her in.


Desire stabs the heart,
the soul,
her approach imbues them.
Fear and uncertainty embrace me.
I am shaken,
unnerved.


Her eyes indite upon my mind,
carved tenets,
'passion' and 'need'.
I am set afire,
eternally.
Oh, how I adore such reverence.


She stops before me,
a lilting voice,
polite regard.
All thoughts vanish,
save one,
".....hhhiii."

# 'MADE FOR EACH OTHER,' 2020

LOVE, a many colorful harmony,
like a beautiful timeless rhapsody,
its feral touch, a savage tempest,
a symphony born of epic tragedy.

HATE, a diversely wicked foe,
akin to a malignant drug,
its essence felt, a shared season,
a gifted charm wrought by love.

# 'THE SEVEN REDES,' 2004

1) Let your word be your bond, and carve it upon thy soul.

2) Be the words you speak, and they will precede you.

3) Proffer nothing less than Integrity, Nobility, Valor, Hospitality, and Justice for all.

4) Expect nothing less than Honor, Solidarity, Ambition, and Fortitude in return.

5) Live by the Rede, and it will Honor you.

6) Serve Justice upon those who defile morality.

7) Be in harmony with those you love, and they will bless you with Fidelity.

# 'LIVING DENIAL,' 2021

I am trapped between the shadows of two worlds, where the candle of life is shaded by a palette of disrepute. Its eidos emanates from the mirror of dissolution, a pridefulness that's tethered by hypocrisy. I cannot pass beyond the gates of reflection, as my own hands have woven the walls of my interment. Fight as I may against the fiends harrying my mind, I am but a captive of pretentious indifference. Is it my destiny to suffer beneath the lash of disparity as I live in denial?

Visions of emptiness plague my mind, a treasonous disease that bredes my soul. I cannot feel its subtle caress nor hear its quate scream. I am but an empty vessel, a hollow shell of a vagrant past. Its essence has abandoned me to an unknown path, one fashioned by the sands of time. The storm it breeds is but the beginning of the tempest that fuels my need. The madness that fills this reliquary is bound to a realm of incivility, one ruled by the unruly domain of self-terrorism. Is it my fate to feel the cut of shattered dreams, those created by living in denial?

Strangers condemn me, judge me, without knowledge or disguise, yet they know not the freedom of verity. I am castigated for a frailty others dream of embracing, yet fear the condemnation of open engagement. To live in the shadows of shame and pressured restraint is nothing more than slavery of the mind. No one should abide its tyrannical rule, as its guise is woven by those who indulge in such vices, secretly, yet denounce others who dare to be bold and viewed as the antithesis of virtue. Is it my fortune to exist unseen, to continue living in denial?

Pardon me for your shortsightedness and the disgrace you feel for your own impure and vagrant thoughts, for I am not the enemy but an extension of our collective conscience. I am the menace you deride, the echoes of disparity you paint on the walls of your own private keep. Oh, how equal lies the sentiment of dissolution among the free and the repressed. Its shadow moves the same in the light as it does in the dark, yet when unseen - hidden from judging eyes - the wickedness of fantasy becomes the libation of greed. Is it my lot to hide such shame, to continue living a life of denial?

Be not afraid with flights of fancy or taboo dreams, for such measures are an indulgence of choice, a fantastic journey to escape the realistic realism of reality. You, who castigate others for your own frailty and faults, bring not wholeness to the quiddity of life but sacrifice all that is free in a world woven by the skein of eternity. You, who deny what is, can never attain the true level of transcendence that creates a trust in those who die - moment to moment - for that which desire contrives as pleasures of the mind, body, and soul. Is it my bane to exist by another's cut, a denial to live as I wish?

Tell me, my friends, my tribe, my species...will we ever deign to be free and let truth bind us to the echoes of the promise given to us by the universe? We should desire to be stronger than the shame that runs through us and push the boundaries of propriety that restrain the pleasures of life, those denied by the vain, the selfish, the hypocrite, and the tyrannical. We are not the pebbles tossed in the pond, but the waves of time that wash ashore, ripple by ripple, like the fading darkness that gives way to the light, shade by shade. Is it our lot to be the victims of living in denial?

So, ask this of yourself - Are you free...or are you a slave to another's mind?

# 'SISTER,' 2002

When I was young, back in the day,
I did not know what it meant,
to be a brother and have a sister,
or know it was a compliment.

There are words I did not say,
and things I wish you knew,
for being there despite my actions,
your brother's love is a thank you.

A sister is one that's tried and true,
a friend beyond compare,
the ties that bind siblings together,
is a bond only family can share.

So, believe the words I pen today,
and know they come from the heart,
my thoughts are always with you,
no matter what keeps us apart.

# 'BROTHER,' 2002

Back in the day, when I was young,
there were things I never knew,
what it meant to be a brother,
or to have one such as you.

There are things I wish you knew,
and things I should have said,
but I can tell you now,
a better brother I could have been.

A brother is one that's always there,
a friend that's tried and true,
one that will always love you,
no matter what you do.

So, with these words, let me say,
these things I did not see,
and believe me when I say this,
you're the only brother I need.

# 'SOUVENIRS,' 2017

The dusky ashes of mourning's war
descend to kiss the savage stage,
an orphic shroud inhuming time
beneath a veil of undying rage.


Upon the fields of crimson glory
rest the souls of woeful memory,
a quate refuge granting solace
to the victims of mortal tragedy.


The standing stones of remembrance
crowd the mead with silent prayers,
rueful missives carved by the living
to bless the dead beyond their years.

# 'BUILT TO SHINE,' 2022

{Part 2}

Beyond the verge of existence where immortals dwell,
I was wrought from the dark like an ancient spell,
a cosmic essence with a specious brand,
spreading death and destruction with a violent plan.

I am the evil that breeds amidst the world of sleep,
an invisible nightmare of dread and deceit,
a sense, a shadow, a menace unseen,
both chaos and fury burn through my bloodstream.

Life is a force upon which I feed,
to slake the hunger of my insatiable greed,
by the winds of fate and the hands of time,
from the fires of creation, I was built to shine.

# 'F.T.F.I.G.L.' 2023

F-is for the fellowship fostered by faith,
R-is for the reverence remembered with grace.
I-is for the idyllic innocence we invocate,
E-is for the evangelical embodiment we incarnate.
N-is for the nature nurtured by Nativity,
D-is for the devout disciples of the Trinity.
S-is for the sacred sanctity we share,
H-is for the holy houses of prayer.
I-is for the intrinsic ideals of intrepidness,
P-is for the passionate prayers of forgiveness.
T-is for the tenets taught by testimony,
H-is for the hallowed hearts of sanctimony.
R-is for the Redeemer's revival by reveille,
O-is for the ordained offering for humanity.
U-is for the ultimate umbrella of unity,
G-is for the garden granted by serenity.
H-is for the hope harbored in heaven,
F-is for the fidelity fostered by Communion.
A-is for the Angels awaiting our arrival,
I-is for the instructions inhabiting the Bible.
T-is for the tacit tablets of testament,
H-is for the healing hands if sacrament.
I-is for the immaculate infant of inspiration,
N-is for the noble Nazarene of Revelation.
G-is for the guidance given by grace,
O-is for the only one we embrace.
D-is for the deliverance divined by decree,
S-is for the sacrificial seal of amnesty.
L-is for the living ledger of law,
O-is for the obligatory ordinance without flaw.
V-is for the vigilant values of virtue,
E-is for the everlasting endowment we pursue.

# 'CONSTELLATIONS,' 2023

A single smile without a mask,
a dozen tears without a laugh.
A hundred hopes without a choice,
a thousand fears without a voice.
A million dreams without a sign,
a billion kisses without a fine.
A trillion frowns without a grin,
a zillion wishes without a djinn.


A single oath without a deed,
a dozen prayers without a creed.
A hundred truths without a lie,
a thousand dares without a try.
A million grifts without a con,
a billion rights without a wrong.
A trillion sins without a cross,
a zillion fights without a loss.


A single belief without a season,
a dozen gods without a reason.
A hundred souls without a faith,
a thousand frauds without a trace.
A million angels without a wreath,
a billion devils without a leash.
A trillion saints without a flaw,
a zillion rebels without a cause.

A single jest without care,
a dozen sighs without despair.
A hundred echoes without pain,
a thousand cries without shame.
A million laughs without meaning,
a billion slurs without feeling.
A trillion jokes without profanity,
a zillion cures without calamity.

A single moment without time,
a dozen rhythms without rhyme.
A hundred habits without style,
a thousand victims without trial.
A million stories without tragedy,
a billion thoughts without depravity.
A trillion wins without hate,
a zillion locks without escape.

A single night without stars,
a dozen days without scars.
A hundred clouds without showers,
a thousand leis without flowers.
A million streams without paddles,
a billion reigns without battles.
A trillion riddles without clues,
a zillion chains without dues.

# 'PROVIDENCE IN PRUSSIA,' 2023

(Inspired by my Friend Linda Mack)

It is said in ages past
constant faith is all we need,
but without the bonds of comradery,
fellowship cannot breed.


Love forms when friendships grow
a haven created within the heart,
the walls harboring its bountiful power
comfort our souls when we're apart.


In our lives, we are taught
how life is all but vanity,
but nothing can prepare the mind
for the loss of love to tragedy.


By the glory of hope and love
and the power of our faith,
all will stand a constant vigil
until granted our rightful place.


The spirit comes when it knows
and shares with us its essence,
the graceful touch of love divine
bestowed by God's presence.

There is a place beyond the clouds
a sacred palace among the blue,
its golden gates are open wide
to the kingdom made for you.

Love and friendship, be it woven
by the faithful in King of Prussia,
all those awaiting the second coming
and the grace of the Messiah.

# 'APERCU', 2019

The breath of life beyond its measure
where the crucible of fire forges creation,
its charm braids the path of Providence
a kingdom devised by time's equation.

The soughing whispers between the stars
be the fading echoes of ages past,
a poet's lament to mark the mourning
of mortal gods consumed by wrath.

The footsteps of eternity build the future
they feed the river, fueling the present,
it fills the gallery of ancient memory
decorating the halls with enduring sentiment.

The wheel of fate turns the glass
to shift the complement of fading sand,
the grains flowing between the rift
destiny tallies with a callous hand.

The blade of death has no tether
its brutal touch bears its kiss,
the cold cut of its savage edge
severs the ties of what exists.

# 'I AM...' 2010

I am the hero upon the stage,
the villain on every page.
I am the rhythm within the song,
the daedal rhyme gone wrong.
I am the cast within the die,
the deepest cut within the lie.
I am the wish in every well,
the poison in every pill.
I am the child of a star,
the stigma of a memoir.
I am the whisper from creation,
the utterly useless predacean.
I am the master of my domain,
the slayer of my name.
I am the husband of every wife,
the worst thing in her life.
I am the flower in every garden,
the mistake without a pardon.
I am the truth once it's spoken,
the devil after it's broken.
I am the divine made whole,
the curse woven from Sheol.
I am the life beyond reason,
the virus of every season.

# 'IMAGENIGMA,' 2016

The shine of sun-dreams,
pleasant remembrance,
full of life and beauty.
Echoes of madness,
captive in the mind,
a colorful seeding,
be chaos and fire,
Its violent touch,
wild as the sea,
tuff as nails,
ever alone,
but free.
I am,
me.
C!
me.
I be,
ego-free.
Ever alone,
quately wild,
like a feral sea,
Its violent touch,
is chaos set afire.
Its bountiful feeling,
clouding up my mind,
the resounding echoes,
filled with life and beauty.
are the shades of memory,
Reflections in the moonshine.

# 'KALEIDOSCOPIC LENS,' 2022

The brush of time strokes keen
it shades the tapestry of our lives,
like banded light through a prism
bringing color to what it rives.


The paint of existence is but the medium
a palette of colors to wash its theme,
a tint to burnish eternal creation
and bring value to its dream.


The pen of age indites slowly
and fashions the epic of our history,
its subtle tones dye the well
to ink the soul with its mystery.


The sands of life wane leisurely
those mortal grains of time's trust,
they spill through the crystal vein
like amber wine made of dust.


The canvas of being waxes swiftly
its hues fade with passing time,
like a shadow chased by the light
beyond the verge of its shine.

# 'NO REASON,' 2023

The thin ledge keeps me,
solid,
unyielding,
beneath trembling knees.
It does not speak,
nor judge,
and will not betray my desire,
a wish for enthasy.

Doubt fills this empty cup,
it robes me of my peace.
Eyes fixed on the asphalt below,
the boulevard of mortal escape
many have known,
intimately.

I want for more,
despair keeps,
a shallow plea for sweet release.
Eyes kiss the sunlit sky,
smiling,
frowning,
pleading,
I am un...afraid.

Clouds gather;
Is it to pray?
I can almost hear their lament.
I wonder if they beseech me to stay,
to fight for undreamt dreams?
Oh, how I wish I knew!

Rains fall,
the sky darkens,
auguring what will surely come.
The end,
the breaking of what is.
A curtain call,
the dénouement...
without a caring friend.

As I step into the open air,
my heart grips with teeth.
It refuses to surrender,
loathing me,
vengeful now,
like a scorned lover.

The ground rushes up,
it reaches skyward to embrace me.
I close my eyes,
feel the rush,
opening my arms to crowded streets.

Onlookers,
gawkers,
hapless peeps,
their careless whispers fill the milieu.
"Tis a shame," they chirp,
"the want of self-defeat."
Alas...my first love lost,
no reason...
but my own.

# 'BLESSED,' 2006

I want for nothing in my life
for thou art always near,
wielding rod and staff
to banish all my fears.

I walk the road of life
without fear or rest,
beside the still waters
of the lake of death.

I am guided by a lamp
along the path, I seek,
your words on my journey
are a light unto my feet.

As I trudge through the valley
plagued by shadows of death,
I feat not the evil
that would steal my breath.

Warnings from the dead
are but things from a dream,
and death is a message
that the soulless bring.

Beyond the shadow's fire
I see the hands of death,
waiting for the time
when I'm not at my best.

The valance of flame
is but a subtle guise,
to trap the innocent
in a web of lies.

Thou art the light
and salvation I seek,
to be my strength
when I become weak.

I hope thee finds me
worthy of thine best,
loves me always
and keeps me blessed.

# 'ENIGMA,' 2006

If I am that which I seek,
but I seek not that I am,
what I am seeks me,
that which seeks me, I shall find.

If I pursue that which I am,
am I not the thing I seek?
And if I find that which I hunt,
will I not be the hound of me?

Are you what I am?
Am I what you are?
If you are that I am,
what I am is you!

If I am what you tell me,
won't you tell me what I am?
If I am what you say,
then what am I to you?

# 'EVEN DUST,' 2020

The whispers betwixt the quate starlight,
hint of mysteries beyond nativity,
of orphic things that once were,
like ancient rhymes lost to memory.

The immortal paeans of creation's Muse,
echo across the ocean of time,
its celestial fires forge anew,
the cosmic eidos of its paradigm.

Conceived in an age beyond remembrance,
forged in the depths of arcane reservoirs,
where the threads of being are born,
from the scattered ashes of quelling stars.

# 'HOPE IS...' 2015

Hope is a candle that burns in the dark,
it fashions the dreams upon which we embark.
Hope is the heart that wishes for more,
the desire of aplomb feeding our core.
Hope is a weapon to defend the heart,
to banish the demons we craft in the dark.
Hope is the meaningful mystery solved,
the joy captured in the rain that falls.
Hope is a passion inspired by the Muse,
a charm of making crafted to imbue.
Hope is the thread to weave the dream,
a colorful tapestry the mind conceives.
Hope is a flame that warms without touch,
like the gold that shines in every rut.
Hope is the essence of Sun and Moon,
it infuses the soul with its copious hue.
Hope is a feeling beyond any need,
a strength to preserve from somewhere deep.
Hope is the charm to enchant the melody,
a song one crafts within their memory.

# 'HATE IS...' 2015

Hate is the crutch of a sour mind,
it feeds the decadence deep inside.
Hate is a weapon loaded with greed,
a vampiric sickness the envious breed.
Hate is the essence of gravid indignation,
immorality that reeks of rabid desperation.
Hate is a prophet that administers blame,
the hollow ambassador of every war game.
Hate is the symptom of a vile disease,
a fanatical indulgence without reprieve.
Hate is a bullet laced with a name,
spit from the muzzle intending to maim.
Hate is the message the jealous decry,
a poisonous pill meant to vilify.
Hate is a knife with a scarlet blade,
the cruelest cut fashioned by rage.
Hate is the purpose to dig a grave,
to bury the enmity of those who enslave.
Hate is a reason that creates a divide,
an absent sentiment fostered by pride.

# 'FEAR IS...' 2015

Fear is a hunter stalking the mind,
creeping closer with the footsteps of time.
Fear is the poison within the pen,
an unctuous residue beneath the skin.
Fear is a demon that leaves its mark,
an indelible essence that rules the dark.
Fear is the scion unable to bloom,
the lifeless blossom trapped in the womb.
Fear is a dungeon where fortitude hides,
a well that drowns the courage inside.
Fear is the edge of a binary blade,
cold as the touch of an empty grave.
Fear is a voice within our head,
the fiend hiding beneath our bed.
Fear is the scourge beyond amnesty,
a plague born of our own insanity.
Fear is a web woven to forbid,
a mental tether contrived by the id.
Fear is the peace we disguise as trust,
camouflage to veil the things we must.

# 'FATE IS...' 2015

Fate is the thread spun by time,
to weave the tapestry of its paradigm.
Fate is a message hidden in the stones,
a mystery revealed as we cast the bones.
Fate is the road with a single path,
a gauntlet for the souls of life's wrath.
Fate is a dictator's license for fear,
an uncomfortable reflection within the mirror.
Fate is the table set from the start,
destiny's menu served a la carte.
Fate is a domain to control the mind,
a fictional realm contrived by the blind.
Fate is the weapon wielded by man,
its feeble measure is counted in sand.
Fate is a path forged by the wind,
no one knows where it will end.
Fate is the pillory to confine the free,
a cell in a prison without a key.
Fate is a star among the sky,
a shining beacon to captivate the eye.

# 'CONCOMITANT,' 2022

Love is a presence we all need,
Hate is a resonance the envious breed.
Choice is a wheel spun by the brave,
Fate is a deil honing its blade.


Hope is a light to vanquish the dark,
Despair is a blight plaguing the heart.
Courage is a pill to give us strength,
Fear is a chill causing restraint.


Honor is a creed carved in stone,
Disgrace is a seed rotten to the bone.
Doubt is a tether woven by fear,
Faith is a treasure meant to share.


Virtue is a quest we seek from birth,
Vice is a test to prove our worth.
Death is a reason to plant a seed,
Life is a season with a temporal deed.


Truth is a bell the righteous ring,
Deceit is a tail with a deadly sting.
Victory is a war won by aggression,
Defeat is a scar left by attrition.

Eternity is an empire without a wall,
Time is a vampire that kills us all.
Diversity is a scale with many faces,
Rhyme is a tale of beautiful phrases.


Trust is a grace we readily guard,
Treason is a face riddled with scars.
Insanity is a plague infecting the mind,
Reason is a shade to color and blind.


Goodness is a battle to strengthen the whole,
Taint is a shadow corrupting the soul.
Sinner is a fable to shame each other,
Saint is a label to crown another.


Absence is a pain most unkind,
Desire is a flame meant to enshrine.
Purity is a form refined with skill,
Fire is a storm to temper our will.


Pain is a price we pay for need,
Pleasure is a spice to pamper our greed.
Work is a goal to help us bloom,
Leisure is a role we all assume.

# 'PICTURE PERFECT,' 2012

Beyond the arc of shaded moon
exists the Eidos of breaking dawn,
within the weaving of its melody
lies the enchantment of its song.


Charming hairstreaks flutter about
floating ornaments of daedal color,
swaying among the prismatic Lea
like poets courting an observant lover.


As I lounge upon a quiet knoll
enjoying the subtle forenoon light,
its essence paints my delicate skin
with the brush of avid delight.


Joyous laughter crowds the air
drifting among the fragrant field,
a child's merriment brings us hope
an ethereal joy of love revealed.


The alpenglow tints the distant horizon
with pastel whispers to shade the sky,
wuthering winds caress the vale
weaving its gift in a subtle lullaby.

# 'FOREVER,' 2003

They say - time can heal any - thing,
but I know - the memories remain.
Even now - that you are gone,
my thoughts of you still linger on.
Here in my heart is forever a love song,
your voice still echoes, even from beyond.
You were the one, my only, forever,
my love, my heart, my always,
forever.

I still feel, the heartache remains,
sowing in my soul, seeds that never fade.
So little time - my love is gone,
to the other side - somewhere beyond.
Sometimes I feel you - in ev-er-y-thing,
hear the wind, whisper your name.
You were the one, my only, forever,
my love, my heart, my always,
forever.

My heart holds on - my faith still remains,
I hold your memory - as the twilight fades.
I close my eyes - pray for grace,
wishing you were here,
kissing tears from my face.
You were the one, my only, forever,
my love, my heart, my always,
forever.
Always together,
tonight, and forever.

Even now - you linger on,
in my heart - where you belong.
I will be strong, my faith will remain,
the hands of time, can't heal my pain.
Here in my heart, even though you're gone,
these thoughts of you,
are forever a love song.

My one, forever,
my love, my heart,
always together,
through the years,
and beyond...forever.

# 'SERENITY,' 2008

The sky emblazoned with starry kiss
paints the morn with aurum shine,
saults of light breach the mist
and floods the land with amber wine.


Rolling waves of swaying grains
and graceful hills of quate majesty,
where purples, blues, and ruby shades
stain the fields with subtle pageantry.


Meadows of orange, greens, and gold
beckon the eyes with pixie delight,
winds of morning flush with cold
heralds the death of passing night.


Turquoise swells braid water and sand
with delicate lace and subtle decor,
the briny deep brings life to land
a host to color the quiet shore.


Winged artisans flutter and play
their chaotic patterns shift and wind,
a courtly dance to charm the day
a dainty waltz cued to time.

# ['ARE WE...' 2021

Are we the strikes of two twelves,
or the proud of its bells?
Are we the prisms to color each other,
or the clouds to shade one another?
Are we the shadow to temper our shine,
or the history built by time?
Are we the riddle within the answer,
or the mystery trapped in the amber?
Are we the clues to our own end,
or the whispers of where we begin?
Are we the vices that feed our greed,
or the pleasures to assuage our need?

Are we the ashes of woven stardust,
or the marques of its trust?
Are we the pearls before the swine,
or the pennies bereft of shine?
Are we the ecstasy in every sigh,
or the poison in every lie?
Are we the shovel that digs the hole,
or the foison that enkindles the soul?
Are we the words that weave the spell,
or the wishes cast in the well?
Are we the thoughts conjured by devils,
or the missives crafted by angels?

Are we the jacks of all trades,
or the amateurs upon the stage?
Are we the poets of every rhyme,
or the provocateurs of every crime?
Are we the apple of every eye,
or the pleas in every cry?
Are we the sacrifice upon the hill,
or the leaves of Yggdrasil?
Are we the message within the bottle,
or the taglines in life's motto?
Are the writing upon the wall,
or the rimes of every snowfall?

Are we the blessings of every sin,
or the crimes against holy doctrine?
Are we the elements that gave us birth,
or the shrines built from the earth?
Are we the song in every chime,
or the cents in every dime?
Are we the salt in every wound,
or the presence in every tomb?
Are we the hope in freedom's call,
or the chains that bind us all?
Are we the grace of divine favor,
or the bane of our creator?

...WHAT WE ARE?]

# 'VAGARY,' 2022

Purpose manifests in a breath of time
a vision of beauty beyond delight,
moments of clarity within disorder
a montage woven of ribbon starlight.

The skein of providence is aurum twine
it knits the bonds of ardent passion,
lacing the heart with gentle pleasures
to weave the mosaic eternity fashions.

Oh, how subtle the breaking morn
the delicate lumen paints my face,
its ethereal nectar fills my soul
with the kiss of mortal grace.

Within the light dwells an essence
an enchanted symphony of esteem,
where soughing souls deign to weave
the threads of immortal dreams.

The cosmos crafts the charms of making
and spins the strands of cogent fate,
to script desires of the heart
upon the tapestry life creates.

Its fiery crucible grooms the spirit
to seek enlightenment beyond reflection,
where odylic whispers conjure life
from the embers of chaotic origin.


Fervid love is the art of war
a mesmeric philter to sway the mind,
the blade of beauty wounds deep
and metes the tears of dying time.

# 'MOMENTS OF SERENITY,' 2007

I desire to explore unknown worlds
and marvel at the wonders of new life,
to purge myself in their immaculate waters
and bathe beneath their immortal light.


I wish to distill the element of hope
from the very heart of eternal fire,
then consume the breath of divine love
and become the essence of infinite desire.


I fight to capture the deepest pose
by the twilit morn I've come to know,
its comforting light imbues the sea
painting its waters an alpenglow.

# 'MARTYR,' 2006

I've felt the hands of destiny weaving the tapestry of my life into a masterpiece of color without flaw. The skein was spun into a coat of many hues that hide my chaotic nightmares among a mirage of blissful dreams. As I watched fate fashion the canvass of my future, I knew then time was formless, and separated my life like sunlight falling through a prism.

I despaired not, as the world whispered a sinister melody to malevolent shadows lying in wait with eager hands to extinguish the candle of my life. Yet, a single stroke from my novice hand changed its vibrant pattern into a sea of woe, as I first drank from the chalice of misery. I knew then "Service is the price we pay for living," *and my shadow is the only one that knows all the dues I've paid.

(*Muhammad Ali)

# 'N.I.K.M.' 2024

A- is for the arresting vision of desire,
B- is for the beauty dressed to inspire.
C- is for the color shading the sky,
D- is for the destiny cast by the die.
E- is for the essence feeding the dream,
F- is for the formula contriving its theme.
G- is for the grace infusing the soul,
H- is for the heart that paves the road.
I- is for the innocent thoughts we carry,
J- is for the journey beyond the cemetery.
K- is for the kinship fostered by faith,
L- is for the love we all create.
M- is for the Mother of all mankind,
N- is for the nature of The Ties That Bind.
O- is for the objects of our obsession,
P- is for the price we pay for our passion.
Q- is for the quittance of Beautiful Imperfections,
R- is for the reality of the dreams we envision.
S- is for the sirens' captivating melody,
T- is for the timeless Imperfections of Beauty.
U- is for the uncanny weaving of providence,
V- is for the vision of Daedal Convergence.
W- is for the world in which we are free,
X- is for the Xanadu of Lumen's Quiddity.
Y- is for the yearning of the absent Sun,
Z- is for the zodiac where our epic was spun!

# 'VARIANCE,' 2021

Beneath the calm of any moment
exists the passion of every dream,
where desirous thoughts weave the strands
spun from the cosmic stream.

Behind the whispers of romantic delight
resides the touch of creation's Muse,
her rhythmic song enchants the heart
to bathe the soul with nature's hues.

Beyond the breaking of the morrow
lies the canvas of virgin dawn,
its subtle brush shades the day
as the drapes of night are drawn.

Between the memories of vanishing time
rests the shades of daedal life,
waiting beyond the candle's halo
is the shadow's shroud to consume the light.

Within the boundary of mortal life
abides the desire of creation unseen,
its delicate beauty is but a mirage
to weave comfort within the dream.

Among the dark where stillness dwells
harks the herald of absent light,
among the quate resides its ballad
a solemn dirge to console the night.

Oh, how drifts a captive whisper
across the ocean of eternal time,
its cryptic ode charms the wind
and calms the waves of an angry mind.

# 'A MERISTIC QUITTANCE,'

(For my Kin) '**2024**'

Eternity's bounty is the breath of being,
an essence conducting its mortal symphony,
within the domain of eternal time,
dwells the Imperfections of Beauty.


Freedom is a light beyond what's seen,
a fragment formed by depraved captivity,
its hope is conjured by a dream,
a paradise born - of Lumen's Quiddity.


Creation's loom be life unbound,
its tangled web is wrought by time,
hallowed hands weave the threads,
to braid The Ties That Bind.


Sentient awareness is a hollow dungeon,
an illusory state of ornamental deception,
it forges the fount of fallow cruelty,
and the charms - of Beautiful Imperfections.


Transient absence breeds infinite desire,
a woeful state of captive suspense,
its grievous touch will slowly fade,
at the advent - of Daedal Convergence.

# Author Bio

T.C. Monk is an artist who excels in multiple mediums. His talents are self-taught, honed during a lengthy prison sentence. During his incarceration, he has spent much of his time educating himself in prose, poetry, ink-and-pencil art, history, ethics, language, philosophy, psychology, theology, and the interconnectedness of family and relationships.

Courtesy, honesty, fidelity, trust, respect, Honor, patience, hospitality, perseverance, and sacrifice are all traits he has fought to instill in himself in hopes of not only creating something out of a broken existence but also proving that with dedication, discipline, and determination, anyone can change their life for the better; all they need to do is try.

Being in prison did not teach him anything of value, as its establishment is absolutely flawed and not built for teaching, correction, or rehabilitation. It is simply a place to warehouse human beings so the prison industry can profit from their sweat and labor. He believes that going to prison may have saved his life and offered him the opportunity to dedicate himself to contriving something better for it. He realized that one can either use the time they are saddled with to benefit themselves or, as many others in prison do, let themselves waste away... never to leave their mark on the world.

Direct messaging with the author is available either through email @ www.securustech.net[1] (using his name and ID #) or

---

1. http://www.securustech.net

snail mail at Arizona Department Of Corrections, Rehabilitation and Reentry, Timothy C. Monk ADCRR #068675, Eyman Complex/Browning Unit, P.O. Box 211309, Dallas, Texas 75211

# Don't miss out!

Visit the website below and you can sign up to receive emails whenever T.C. Monk publishes a new book. There's no charge and no obligation.

https://books2read.com/r/B-A-TGZAB-OEUTC

BOOKS 2 READ

Connecting independent readers to independent writers.

2. https://books2read.com/u/bwA7oG

3. https://books2read.com/u/bwA7oG

restraint, and unnatural shadows. Compiled over more than 20 years, this collection serves as a cartography—both intellectual and emotional—of one man's search for wisdom, truth, and peace.

His poetry is deliberate; every word and image is carefully chosen. Monk's poems are not for those who are easily intimidated or who seek poetry that requires no effort to read. They are neither purely cerebral nor spontaneous eruptions of powerful feelings. Nor are they mere rhymes meant as an end in themselves, nor a chaotic landscape of words and letters scattered haphazardly into the wind to land and sprout independently. Instead, the poems are meticulously crafted. They form a scaffold upon which Monk constructs a spiritual lighthouse—a place to muse, imagine, create, conjecture, and conjure incantations and songs, as well as an effort to explore and transcend dimensions of time, space, and spirit. In doing so, he lays bare not only the shadow and light of his own soul but also the essential human spirit that binds us all. His poems teach us about our shared humanity, showing that what we love, fear, hate, and desire are inextricably intertwined. In their relative proximity, these emotional dimensions of our lives reveal our fragility even as they stand as a testament to human resilience.

www.ingramcontent.com/pod-product-compliance
Lightning Source LLC
Chambersburg PA
CBHW072033150726
47999CB00002B/884